FOUR
WHEEL DRIVE

FOUR
WHEEL DRIVE
OFF ROAD, OFF LIMITS

NIGEL FRYATT AND GRAHAM SCOTT

CHARTWELL
BOOKS, INC.

A QUINTET BOOK

Published by Chartwell Books
A Division of Book Sales, Inc.
PO Box 7100
Edison, New Jersey 08818-7100

This edition produced for sale in the U.S.A, its
territories and dependencies only.

ISBN 0-7858-0313-0

This book was designed and produced by
Quintet Publishing Limited
6 Blundell Street
London N7 9BH

CREATIVE DIRECTOR: *Richard Dewing*
DESIGNER: *Simon Balley*
SENIOR PROJECT EDITOR: *Stefanie Foster*
EDITOR: *Kit Coppard*

Typeset in Great Britain by
Central Southern Typesetters, Eastbourne
Manufactured by Eray Scan Pte Ltd, Singapore
Printed by Star Standard Industries (Pte) Ltd, Singapore

CONTENTS

What is the appeal of 4WD?

ABOVE

From its initial conception, the Land Rover has been seen as an authentically British vehicle. Prime Minister Winston Churchill stands with one of the earliest models oustide his *Chartwell residence. And it seems personalized registration plates were obviously all the rage in the 1940s since this is an early 80 in. wheelbase model, and a British product.*

Flick the clock back a mere 100 years to the birth of the automobile. Its introduction revolutionized personal, as well as commercial, transportation. There were some extraordinary, forward-thinking engineers at the time; they would have been intrigued and impressed today with how far automotive technology has progressed over a relatively short period. It is easy to forget, however, that the automobile would never have gotten this far without the

development of the infrastructure – without roads. From early rough tracks to multilane super highways, the great majority of automobiles still need roads. Vehicles with four-wheel drive (4WD) do not.

If the automobile opened our eyes to the benefits of mass transportation, the 4WD vehicle has opened our minds – paradoxically, both by stretching our horizons and making it possible for us to reach them. The 4WD has all the benefits of the standard automobile, with the added "go anywhere" ingredient that makes it so very special.

Yet the glamorous aura of the present-day 4WD must not be allowed to obscure the humdrum circumstances of its origins. Necessity is the mother of invention, and it was the need to move military personnel around the battlefields of Europe that inspired the design of the Willys Jeep, the best-known of the early, light utility 4WDs to be mass-produced.

VITAL STATISTICS		
	1948 WILLYS JEEP	**LAND-ROVER**
WHEELBASE:	80in. (2030mm)	80in. (2030mm)
WIDTH:	62in. (1575mm)	60in. (1525mm)
LENGTH:	133in. (3380mm)	132in. (3355mm)
TRACK:	48in. (1220mm)	50in. (1270mm)
ENGINE:	4-cylinder 2.1-liter (128cu.in.) 60bhp at 3600rpm	4-cylinder 1.6-liter (98cu.in.) 55bhp at 4000rpm
WEIGHT:	2315lb. (1050kg)	2520lb. (1143kg)

A 1947 Land Rover prototype. It is worth noting the unique central seat design that was converted to a more conventional layout before the vehicle went into production.

Birth of the Land Rover

The American Jeep was the first, but it was a British company that took hold of the Jeep concept, went into peace-time production, and launched and then developed the 4WD market as we know it today.

Back in 1948, Maurice Wilks was a director of the British Rover company; he also owned a farm in Anglesey, North Wales, and a Willys Jeep – one of many left behind in Britain by the US Army after World War II. Wilks was very impressed by the Jeep's potential as an agricultural vehicle, and it was to

influence his decision on future models. However, immediately after the war, a shortage of steel was having a major effect in limiting the British car manufacturers from returning to full production of civilian models. Wilks, therefore, turned his ideas into producing a limited production run of what could be called a British "Jeep." A glance at the accompanying table shows that the first Land-Rover (originally the name was hyphenated) was a very close copy indeed.

Some 45 years later, some things have changed and some remain the same. Land Rover (now without the hyphen) is the most successful sole 4WD manufacturer in the world, with an enviable reputation for some of the toughest "go anywhere" vehicles ever built. The company's line includes the agricultural, commercial, and military vehicles which all remain remarkably similar to that original design. But this choice now extends to the Range Rover and Discovery, two vehicles in the public marketplace that many claim are unchallenged in their off-road ability. Land Rover will proudly tell you that the latest Range Rover, introduced in mid-1994, is simply the best mass-produced 4WD in the world.

The Jeep Reborn

The Jeep name hasn't disappeared, either. Now meeting great sales success in both the U.S. and Europe in the guise of the Cherokee and Grand Cherokee, the name is also on the Wrangler, a product that remains proud of its "original" military looks – albeit now painted in bright body colors rather than military khaki, and boasting wide wheels, megawatt stereo systems, and driven by bright young things rather than servicemen.

BELOW
Given their matching specifications, it is of little surprise that the first Land Rovers look similar to the Willys Jeep. Pictured here is a 1941 MA Jeep complete with sturdy front bumper and token wet-weather protection.

*Land Rover designer
Maurice Wilks was
himself a farmer, and this
picture of the 1947 central
seat prototype could well
have been taken at his
North Wales farm.*

Extremes of Purpose

Four-wheel drives have played their part in many
global conflicts. Yet while the Land Rover owes much
to the Willys Jeep – Land Rover's chief designer
Maurice Wilks both owned and admired the
American vehicle – the British four-wheel drive was
firmly aimed at being of use to farmers as a serious
agricultural machine. Prototype jeeps had less
altruistic intentions. One of the first, designated the
"Blitz Buggy," was tested by Colonel (later General)
Dwight D. Eisenhower. The production models were
of great assistance to the Allies in the European
World War II effort.

*The demands of the
military have led to the
development of the
monstrous Hummer four-
wheel drives (described on
page 70). This desert
Hummer is of the type
used in the Gulf War.*

*The extreme work that
Jeeps were expected to
perform during World
War II meant that chains
were sometimes fitted to
the tires for extra traction.*

This schematic drawing shows clearly how the engine at the front can be made to drive all four of the vehicle's wheels. The drawing is of a Mercedes-Benz G-Wagen, but the principles can be used for the majority of production based four-wheel drives.

Two-wheel drive: Many 4WD vehicles have the option of running in two-wheel drive, when on dry paved roads, for instance. Drive from the engine is therefore transferred along the rear drive shaft (6) to the rear differential (7) and rear axle (8). An off-road vehicle is then running in the same way as a standard rear-wheel drive automobile.

Four-wheel drive: When the driver engages four-wheel drive, he brings the vehicle's transfer box (5) into operation. This is effectively the vehicle's second transmission and is therefore what makes the difference between standard road cars and off-road machines. The transfer box now allows drive from the engine through the main transmission and divides it along both the rear and the front (4) drive shafts, to their respective differentials (1 and 7) and axles. Both the rear, and the front wheels, are now turning under power from the engine.

High and Low ratio: The transfer box itself has two sets of ratios. High and Low, which work in series with the main transmission. A vehicle with a standard five-speed transmission therefore has five in High ratio (for normal road driving) and five in Low ratio (for difficult off-road terrain).

Key

1. FRONT DIFFERENTIAL
2. FRONT AXLE
3. DRIVE FROM ENGINE AND MAIN TRANSMISSION
4. FRONT DRIVE SHAFT
5. TRANSFER BOX
6. REAR DRIVE SHAFT
7. REAR DIFFERENTIAL
8. REAR AXLE

Escape from the Blacktop

Of course, the latest people to come to the 4WD party have been the Japanese. This is an understandable move, given this highly competitive country's worldwide success in both motorcycle and conventional car production. Once again, the Japanese have first imitated and then innovated with their 4WD products, increasing what is on offer for the consumer.

Why have drivers, both in America and western Europe, taken to 4WD with such unbridled enthusiasm? The answer to that question is difficult to state simply, but will be found in the pages of words and pictures of this book. The 4WD vehicle allows people to be different; it allows people to take off from the asphalt of the urban jungle and explore the most rugged countryside far from the madding crowd. Or at least it offers that potential, that chance to dream.

Today's 4WD machines are eminently capable of traveling over some amazingly severe terrain, and we cover this more fully elsewhere in the book. They have also inspired the development of a whole new area of motorsport, with high-speed thrills across the rough stuff that appeals both to participants and spectators. More important, however, 4WDs are fun to live with; practical, certainly; but with enormous enjoyment potential . . . .

LEFT
Today, four-wheel drive is a family affair; this five-door Suzuki Vitara JX is an excellent example of one of the most popular small 4WD vehicles in the world.

The Way Ahead

And what of the future? Well, just by looking at the models we have collected here, that future appears pretty healthy. The space-age designs of the Renault Racoon, Jeep ECCO, and the Isuzu XU-I are only the tip of the iceberg, yet they do show how firmly rooted is the belief in the future of 4WD. Renault, for instance, despite their flirtation with AMC some years back, has not been known for its 4WD products, yet here is the Racoon promoting the French manufacturer off the road. And the Jeep, the name that started it all, remains up front with the ECCO. The Isuzu XU-I, despite its Japanese heritage, was designed at the Technical Center of

Even the Italian supercar manufacturer Lamborghini has previously dabbled with the 4WD concept, producing this rather functional-looking LM500. Despite its luxury interior, V12 engine, and rich Arab owners, it is really something of an aged rocker and is no longer in production.

LEFT

And what of the future? Many manufacturers new to four-wheel drive have interesting projects in the pipeline. This is the Racoon from Renault.

Jeep can justifiably claim to be one of the manufacturers that started the mass production of light utility four-wheel drives, and the company's design engineers remain as enthusiastic as ever with the concept, as this Jeep ECCO clearly demonstrates.

Perhaps not the most functional 4WD design, the Renault Racoon is a fully working design study that caused quite a stir at international motor shows.

America in Cerritos, California. The men behind the computers in the design studio claim to have been influenced by the Lockheed Stealth bomber, showing that the creators of some 4WDs continue to draw inspiration from military technology. The XU-1 (sounds rather like a plane, doesn't it?) also has a CD-ROM graphics computer system offering the occupants three-dimensional topographical navigation maps, as well as video and stereo music systems. Beats using a road map and pocket compass, I guess.

And in case you think that futuristic machines never make it into production, check out the latest small 4WD, the RAV4 from Toyota. This neat little machine evolved from a dramatic concept vehicle that was first seen at the Tokyo Motor Show and is now in a downtown showroom near you.

The world of 4WD is just getting started.

LEFT

Despite its Isuzu name plate, the XU-1 was designed in California and has been influenced by the Lockheed Stealth bomber. Off-road in extremis, indeed.

CHAPTER
2
the top ten
The World's Best Production 4WDs

RANGE ROVER

4.6-liter HSE

The finest 4WD in the world?

BELOW

The lines echo the Classic Range Rover, but are all-new. What is remarkable is how similar it looks, given that 99% of all components are new.

The Range Rover has always had a rather tough up-bringing because it was so dramatically different from the other more workaday and rugged vehicles in the Land Rover catalog. It offered comfort and refine-ment and, as the years rolled by, moved ever closer to the luxury car market. Of course, real Land Rovers, while they now have a nodding acquaintance with comfort, are basically agricultural: their virtues are ultimate mud-plugging ability and structural integrity. But the Range Rover, even as it becomes ever more luxurious (and expensive), has not forgotten its heritage: it continues to be one of the world's greatest off-road machines.

ABOVE

A 4.0 liter (244 cu.in.) SE in its element. A quick power-wash and it can be cruising at 90mph on the autobahn.

RIGHT

The 4.0-liter V8 SE sits between the 2.5-liter (152.5 cu.in.) BMW-engined turbo-diesel and the brand-topping 4.6-liter (289 cu.in.)V8 HSE.

Evolution, Not Gimmicks

Significant as they are, the latest changes to the Range Rover's exterior preserve the vehicle's basic shape, while demonstrably improving it in a number of important details.

Beneath the skin, too, it is a story of steady engineering development rather than any dramatic change. The golden rule of 4WD design – established by Land Rover – for a separate chassis onto which you fit the body, is maintained; the latest Range Rover has its ladder-frame chassis strengthened to meet new American car-crash testing standards. The Electronic Air Suspension system is retained; but this time, after more development research on the vehicle's behavior at speed on the asphalt, its normal road height has been lowered to improve high-speed stability.

Power is traditional, with Range Rover still using the V8 unit based on the Buick block. From the

TOP TEN SPECIFICATION:
RANGE ROVER

ENGINE:
All-aluminum V8 gasoline with self-adjusting hydraulic tappets and fully electronic management system

CAPACITY OPTIONS:
4.0-liter (244 cu.in.), 4.2-liter (256 cu.in.), 4.6-liter (289 cu.in.)

TRANSMISSION:
Five-speed manual with two-speed full-time transfer case. Or four-speed automatic with two-speed full-time transfer case

SUSPENSION:
FRONT: *Variable-rate air-springs with beam axle, anti-roll bar, radius arms, and Panhard rod*
REAR: *Variable-rate air-springs with beam axle, composite trailing link, and Panhard rod*

STEERING:
Power-assisted recirculating ball

BRAKES:
Ventilated front and solid rear disks with ABS

original European specification of 3.5 liters (215 cu.in.), the engine remains with only two valves per cylinder and single overhead camshafts, but has been stretched to offer three options: 190bhp 4.0-liter (244 cu.in.); a 200bhp 4.2-liter (256 cu.in.); and now a bore-busting 4.6-litre (289 cu.in) pumping out 225bhp. A strong push behind this seemingly endless capacity growth has to be the need to sell Range Rovers in North America, yet one wonders how long Land Rover's new owners BMW will resist the temptation to install a high-tech, multivalve engine designed in the 1990s – like the German company's own V8 or V12 options, for instance.

Big, unstressed engine, everything controlled by electronics, a luxurious interior – but that chassis and suspension set this apart from all the other luxury sedans on the road.

The new interior, an enviable place to be. It is a vast improvement on the old interior, particularly ergonomically.

Electronic Wizardry

The electronic systems within the Range Rover are mind-numbingly complex. The GEMS (Generic Engine Management System) monitors everything that is happening under the hood, while linking to the BeCM (Body electronic Control Module) which monitors just about everything else, from the vehicle's ride height to whether the windshield washer bottles are empty.

Mud-Plugging in Luxury

Letting the vehicle's brain sort out exactly what is happening under the skin allows the driver to revel in the rumbling V8 and in a machine which is significantly better on road than ever before. Land Rover makes no bones of the fact that they see this Range Rover as a top-quality luxury car competing with Mercedes, Audi, and BMW sedans. The difference is, of course, the option with the Range Rover to take this air-conditioned, luxury people-carrier deep into the most stinking mud hole you can find with supreme confidence – if only because you will undoubtedly employ other people to clean it up for you afterward.

LAND ROVER DISCOVERY V8i AUTOMATIC

Solid integrity and modern grace

It could be confidently asserted that Land Rover was forced into producing the Discovery. After all, the company had for many years enjoyed total domination of the commercial 4WD market. One of the Land Rover's most important qualities has been its ability to evolve without seeming to change at all. Thus the basic design could be transformed into longer-wheelbase versions, ambulance versions, agricultural pickup versions, personnel carriers, even cross-country gunships, to name but a few. At the other end of the scale, Land Rover developed the Range Rover, pushing that model further and further upscale and up in price.

Filling the Model Gap

It doesn't take a highly-paid automobile industry analyst to spot the gap that opened between these two extremes and grew ever wider. And as the popularity of 4WD increased, so there developed a market of people who wanted 4WDs with more comfort and road-going characteristics than the traditional Land Rover, at a price considerably lower than that of a new Range Rover. Other manufacturers had already noticed this and were quick to put suitable models into production. Eventually, Land Rover was roused – and the result, in 1988, was the Discovery.

The Discovery's appearance owes much to both the solid integrity of the Land Rover and the more modern grace of the Range Rover. From every angle, this is obviously a serious off-roader, but also a vehicle with on-road class and distinction.

The Discovery's reputation has been much enhanced by its participation in one of the world's toughest off-road events, the Camel Trophy. This is a turbo-diesel version in the 1991 event.

When it finally appeared, the criticism that it had taken the company so long to produce it melted away. So good was this mid-range 4WD that the demand for models threatened to overrun Land Rover. Extra shifts were organized, even a night shift – something that had not been seen for many a long year.

Family Features

The Discovery is standard Land Rover through and through. Separate ladder-frame chassis – the same size as that of the original Range Rover – onto which is secured a stylish body. Thankfully, this styling reflects its bigger Range Rover brother rather than the down-on-the-farm, agricultural cousin.

For the European markets, the Discovery has a variety of engine options from 2-liter (122 cu.in.), four-cylinder gasoline to a 2.5-liter (152.5 cu.in.) turbo-diesel unit. Top of the list of options, however, has to be the 3.9-liter (238 cu.in.) V8 available in three- or five-door body styles, with five-speed manual or four-speed automatic transmission.

As you would expect, the Discovery has superb off-road manners, thanks again to that Land Rover suspension philosophy. Long wheel travel is allowed by coil springs all around and the recognizable trailing link and A-frame set-up at the rear.

Ample Power

The V8 engine, pushed out to its 3.9-liter (238 cu.in.) capacity, is large by European standards, although rather more "average" when compared to other options on the American market. Relatively unsophisticated, with only two valves per cylinder and single overhead camshaft, it still provides 180bhp of glorious V8 rumble. The four-speed automatic transmission is ideally suited to both the V8 and installation in the Discovery, offering sprightly on-road performance and the agility off-road that you would expect from a Land Rover powered by a high-

ABOVE

To meet market demands, the Discovery now has a much improved interior; fully leather trimmed and fitted with air-bags to satisfy North American customers.

torque V8 engine. Using an automatic transmission off-road requires a slightly different driving technique, but the Discovery is unlikely to be found lacking.

Having proved a major success in Europe, the V8 Discovery ended 1994 being sold in Japan as the Honda Crossroad and looking set to conquer the North American market. It may have been a long time coming, but the Discovery has already carved itself a significant niche in the world of 4WD.

LAND ROVER

DEFENDER

90 V8

An unmistakable classic

This is obviously a Land Rover, but recent market trends have seen the addition of more creature comforts for driver and passenger alike.

There are some unwritten, but well-understood, rules about driving a 4WD off-road. One of these relates to engines or, more specifically, to their size. In off-road driving, it most definitely is a case where size matters – as well as the driver's ability to exploit that large capacity to the full.

There are many enthusiasts on both sides of the Atlantic for whom the V8 engine is the only option for those demanding real off-road performance. There is an even larger number of enthusiasts around the world for whom a Land Rover is the only vehicle option for ultimate off-road ability. Taking those views as gospel for the moment, if you combine the two, you will obviously have an exceptional machine.

And that's exactly what you have with the Land Rover Defender 90 V8. It is not particularly comfortable to drive on-road. It is certainly not a modern body design (little has really changed since its 1948 conception). Indeed, there's little to recommend it if city streets are your natural environment. But take this Defender off-road and things are very different.

Is there a 4WD enthusiast who could not recognize a Land Rover Defender? Indeed, it is probably one of the most readily recognized shapes in the history of automobile production.

The modern Land Rover still has the chunky "Tonka-toy" feeling to it that it has always had; the machine gives the impression that with a few big wrenches under your arm, the whole thing could be dismantled and re-assembled with ease.

The boxy look allows for the "one-wheel-at-each-corner" approach, which is essential for a good off-roader. There is very little front or rear overhang of bodywork, which gives it class-leading approach and departure angles. This allows the driver to drop down and climb out of the steepest holes without fear of bending expensive metalwork on rocks or muddy outcrops.

The Defender 90's other major virtue is its superb axle articulation and wheel travel. This allows all four wheels on a Defender to point at different and seemingly impossible angles at the same time, while still retaining firm contact with the ground and therefore able to offer traction to the 4WD system. The vehicle's simple but highly effective coil spring suspension for each wheel connected to the rigid ladder-frame chassis offers a unique combination of agility and structural strength.

Torquey Engine

The V8 engine is similar in specification to that of Discovery V8, which means 3.9-liter (238 cu.in.) and 180bhp. Off-road, however, it is torque that matters – the effective "pulling power" delivered to the wheels when the unit is turning over at relatively low revs. In this case, it's a thumping 233lb/foot at a lazy 3100rpm. That is certainly enough to pull the Defender out of the deepest of scrapes.

It would be difficult to find any other 4WD vehicle that can trace its routes back so far and yet be proud that so little has actually changed. Pretty it is not, but the Land Rover Defender is an unmistakable classic. For anyone who ever has occasion to take 4WDs to the extreme limits of off-road driving, the Land Rover Defender 90 V8 is simply unbeatable.

ENGINE:
All-aluminum V8 gasoline fuel-injected and fully electronic management system

CAPACITY OPTIONS:
3.9-liter (238 cu.in.)

TRANSMISSION:
Five-speed manual with two-speed full-time transfer case

SUSPENSION:
FRONT: *Live axle, radius arms, coil springs, and Panhard rod*
REAR: *Live axle, coil springs, trailing link, and A-frame*

STEERING:
Power-assisted, worm-and-roller

BRAKES:
Ventilated front and solid rear disks with ABS

TOYOTA LAND CRUISER VX

The top Toyota

Toyota's Land Cruiser has had an immense impact on the world of 4WD. And that's appropriate, because it is an immense 4WD truck. In Europe, the Land Cruiser has won the influential *Off Road & 4 Wheel Drive* magazine's prestigious 4x4 Car of the Year award in both 1993 and 1995. And when you consider that this particular award puts the Toyota up against the best that Europe has to offer from the likes of Land Rover, all the top Japanese contenders from Mitsubishi, Isuzu, and Suzuki, together with the North American contender Jeep, you begin to understand the caliber of the achievement.

A Class Act

If asked to comment on one characteristic of the Land Cruiser that has helped to see it attain such heights and stubbornly remain there, it has to be build quality. There is a solid nature to this machine's construction that must make other manufacturers envious.

Add build quality to a lusty engine, which in this case is a six-cylinder, 4.2-liter (256 cu.in.) turbo-charged diesel unit, with a massive torque figure of 265lb/foot at an amazingly low 1800rpm, and it is evident that the Land Cruiser is a class act indeed.

Superb driving position, with a great number of controls all neatly and sensibly laid out. The quality is absolute.

TOYOTA LAND CRUISER VX

ENGINE:
Six-cylinder, in-line, direct injection turbocharged OHC diesel

CAPACITY OPTIONS:
4.2-liter (256 cu.in.) gasoline and 4.2-liter (256 cu.in.) diesel turbo

TRANSMISSION:
Five-speed manual with two-speed full-time transfer case, or four-speed automatic with two-speed full-time transfer case. Lockable center diff. Lockable front and rear cross-axle diffs

SUSPENSION:
FRONT: *Live axle, coil springs plus anti-roll bar*
REAR: *Live axle, coil springs plus anti-roll bar*

STEERING:
Power-assisted recirculating ball

BRAKES:
Ventilated front and solid rear disks with ABS

The rounded lines add grace to bulk, but you can't disguise the sheer size and impact of the vehicle. Few would want to.

ABOVE
Serious stuff. Big chassis, big engine, permanent four-wheel drive, and diff locks front, center and rear all mean business.

It is no secret that the Japanese manufacturer looked long and hard at Land Rover before building its Land Cruiser, and so it is no surprise that the top Toyota boasts a separate chassis, with coil-sprung live axles at front and rear. This allows for the necessary good axle articulation to give the Land Cruiser excellent off-road ability – an ability that often seems to belie the vehicle's obvious bulk.

Transmission Electronics

But the Toyota engineers have not been satisfied with just imitating the Land Rover; they have felt it necessary to innovate as well. This can be seen in the complicated electronic package that the Land Cruiser has designed into its transmission. Beside the transmission options of four-speed automatic or five-speed manual with two-speed full-time transfer case, the Land Cruiser also has a lockable center differential (when in low range) and sequentially engaged locking front and rear cross-axle differentials. These give the driver an assortment of buttons to press when he ventures off-road and, whether necessary or not, they are there, and they work.

The top of the line VX version also has all that one would expect in a luxury machine, but which is not always available on an off-roader, including air-conditioning and high-quality leather trim.

All these luxury extras allow the Land Cruiser to offer its occupants a great deal of comfort during long-distance superhighway cruising. With a gross weight of 6527 pounds (2960kg), even the impressive six-cylinder power unit struggles a bit to make particularly rapid acceleration. Off-road, the performance is there, once the driver has become used to the vehicle's bulk – and which buttons he wants to press to lock which axles!

In Europe, the Land Cruiser's success has been in what it has to offer when compared to the Range Rover. Some say it offers more at a lower price, and that is high praise indeed.

BELOW

Suspension gives flexibility with strength, while anti-roll bars help to control high-speed on-road driving. Leading arms and coil springs at the front combine with four-link rear suspension also with coil springs, both ends with solid axles.

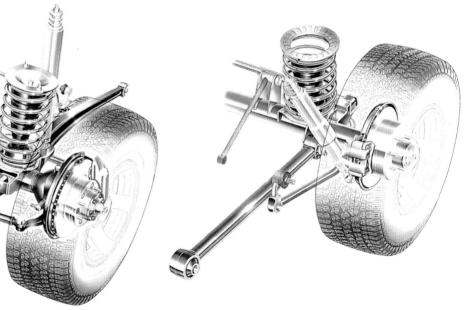

FORD EXPLORER

A lot to offer

Ford's importance in the 4WD market should not be underestimated. In Europe, the Maverick 4WD has begun to establish a firm foothold against the traditional opposition from General Motors and the Far East. If anything, however, the stakes are even higher in the U.S., and to meet this, ol' Henry now has a heavily revised version of the Explorer available.

A new front end and a totally redesigned instrument panel are the obvious visual changes over the previous version, but as in all the best stories, it is only when you dig a little deeper that you find the interesting bits.

The 4-liter (244 cu.in.) V6 engine is a particularly torquey unit, ideal for serious off-roading – or just transporting heavy loads.

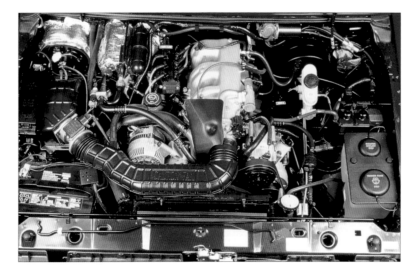

New Power Train

Power for the Explorer, perhaps rather surprisingly, comes from Europe, in the form of the 4.0-liter (244 cu.in.) V6 (known as the Cologne V6). Fuel-injected, this provides the Explorer with unremarkable 160bhp at 4200rpm, but it's the unit's torque that impresses most, delivering 225lb/foot at a leisurely 2800rpm. This is transferred to the wheels via a four-speed automatic transmission with overdrive.

ABOVE

The latest Ford Explorer is visually very similar to its predecessors, but underneath much has been changed, developed, and improved.

TOP TEN SPECIFICATION:
FORD EXPLORER

ENGINE:
Fuel injected V6

CAPACITY OPTIONS:
4.0-liter (244 cu.in.)

TRANSMISSION:
*Five-speed manual with overdrive or four-speed
automatic with overdrive. Control Trac 4WD
system (see text)*

SUSPENSION:
FRONT: *Independent, unequal-length
short and long arms, coil springs*
REAR: *Live axle, coil springs*

STEERING:
Rack-and-pinion

BRAKES:
Disks all around with ABS

ABOVE

A good load area and ability to carry people, luggage, and all the necessary items for your chosen leisure activity is vital for any 4WD's sales success.

Ford's engineers have completely revised the suspension. Gone is the old traditional I-beam system that is used on the pickup, replaced by an independent front end based on unequal length "wishbones," called short and long arms in the United States. This is all coordinated with a complete change in steering; gone is the recirculating ball, replaced by the far more precise rack-and-pinion.

State of the Art Suspension

The chassis is kept in check with an Automatic Ride Control (ARC) system, which is claimed to be unique in this market segment. This system provides a comprehensive damping control of the vehicle's shock absorbers which automatically changes between firm and normal positions, depending on the inputs from the driver (speed, steering, and braking). The ARC also controls the vehicle's ride height; in AERO mode, it lowers the ride height for high-speed interstate work; the CURB mode is for 4WD driving at speeds under 50mph (80kmh); the OFF-ROAD mode raises the height above CURB mode when in low ratio and at speeds under 30mph (48kmh).

Drive Alternatives

The Explorer's Control Trac system is claimed to be the first to be offered in the American sports utility vehicle market. Basically, it offers the driver the choice of 2 or 4WD at the touch of a button on the dashboard. There are three options: 2WD for normal road driving; continuous 4WD for mud-plugging; and the automatic 4WD option. When the Explorer is in automatic 4WD, sensors in both axles are used to detect slippage. When this occurs, the system engages the center differential and so provides drive to the front axle (in 2WD mode, the Explorer drives only the rear wheels).

To make sure all this happens in the smoothest possible manner, the Explorer has a newly designed transfer case incorporating a multiplate clutch device. Gone are the old style lockable front hubs, bringing the Ford Explorer firmly up to the standards of its main competitors. At the vehicle's announcement in late 1994, Ford claimed it would further strengthen the car's best-in-class position. Only time will tell, but the Explorer certainly has a lot to offer.

BELOW
With switches for electric everything, and leather trim just about everywhere, Ford aims for comfort for everyone.

CHEVROLET

BLAZER

More options than in Denny's Diner

This has long been a favorite in the U.S. – and now it's even better. The S-10 Blazer was a mainstay of the compact sports utility sector. Today it is just called the Blazer, without further embellishment of the name. Carrying either the Chevrolet or GMC badge, this vehicle is the product of the rationalization and modernization that has been going on in the North American auto industry during the past few years, a process designed to fend off the Japanese and make people buy American again. It looks like it's working.

BELOW

The revised interior of the latest model Blazer has its fair share of driver comforts – including an outlet for your cellular phone.

Oriental Influence

It has to be said that, for a vehicle designed to withstand the oriental opposition, there is a touch of the Japanese about the styling of the Blazer. It is considerably more aerodynamic than the S-10, although the family resemblance is clear. There's also more interior and luggage space, along with analog dials, supportive front seats, and a much improved dashboard, and safety features include a driver's-side airbag. You even get a 12-volt outlet for cellular phones.

Under the hood there is a powerful 4.3-liter (262 cu.in.) central-port-injection V6 giving 200bhp, which compares very favorably with the old model's 163bhp. With 260lb/foot of torque at 3600rpm, you certainly get enough grunt for both highway and off-road rough stuff.

This is a modern V6 using electronics to keep it clean and lean and is the sort of engine American companies need to be building for the future rather than the massive, gas-guzzling V8s so long favored by the stateside customer.

BELOW
Improved aerodynamics and a more powerful engine give an excellent performance package, on- and off-road.

TOP TEN SPECIFICATION:
CHEVROLET BLAZER

ENGINE:
V6 gasoline with central-port injection

CAPACITY OPTIONS:
4.3-liter (262 cu.in.)

TRANSMISSION:
Five-speed manual or four-speed automatic with part-time two-speed transfer case

SUSPENSION:
FRONT: *Live axle, coil springs, and gas dampers*
REAR: *Live axle, coil springs, gas dampers*

STEERING:
Power-assisted variable-ratio rack-and-pinion

BRAKES:
Ventilated front disks and solid rear disks

Option Package

This being an American vehicle, you get more options than in Denny's Diner. You can have two-door bodywork, manual or automatic transmission, two- or four-wheel drive, option packs, and four suspension packages ranging from base to off-road. About the only item that doesn't have any options is the engine.

Driving a Blazer shows up the many ways in which it has been modernized, giving the benchmark Ford Explorer a serious run for its very reasonable money. With the off-road suspension packs, you get gas-pressurized de Carbon or Bilstein shocks with seriously big stabilizer bars front and rear, along with silver-steel wheels, big tires, and special bump-stops. A new variable-ratio steering rack and revised front-suspension settings combine to greatly enhance straight-line stability. There is none of the "hunting" around the highway you get with some fat-tired off-road vehicles when they hit the blacktop. The wheels track straight and true – and look good, too.

Initially, you could get this specification only with the 4L60-E electronically controlled four-speed auto transmission with overdrive, but a five-speed manual came in early in 1995. Interestingly, the top off-road handling package is available only on the two-door model. But whichever model you choose, the improved aerodynamics of the new shape along with the noticeably more powerful engine give you an excellent performance package on or off the highway and plenty of space for all your gear. The Blazer now fits.

ABOVE

Under the skin of the Chevy Blazer, you can clearly see the drivetrain and the seating layout of what is a very popular American four-wheel drive vehicle. The latest model is considerably more aerodynamic than the previous S-10.

BELOW

Off-roaders always look their best in the rough outdoors, and that's the appeal. Vehicles like the Blazer LT allow you to enjoy the view, not just the photographs.

JEEP CHEROKEE

A box full of goodies

The quality may not be of the highest but all the goodies are there – leather, wood, and air-bag among others.

From one angle, the Cherokee looks like just another two-box 4WD, with a simple and fairly agricultural gasoline engine and unsophisticated suspension. Looked at another way, it emerges as a clever blend of American station wagon, road car, and 4WD, with a distinctively angular shape in contrast to the soft, rounded contours favored by other car and 4WD manufacturers. It is obvious which styling philosophy is closer to current American taste: the Cherokee took the U.S. by storm – and then proceeded to cross the Atlantic and make a hit in Europe. In the 18 months after its launch in Britain, the Cherokee found 8,000 British buyers – modest by American standards, but huge for a new 4WD in Britain.

Jeep has been out of the Australian market for nearly ten years, but now it is back with the Wrangler and Cherokee.

ABOVE

The 4.0-liter (244 cu.in.) Limited SE Cherokee – an American at home in the English woods.

Keeping It Simple

The Japanese have specialized in new shapes, sophisticated suspensions, engines managed by ever more complex electronics, and of course keen prices. The Cherokee is Neolithic by comparison: it has an iron 4.0-liter (244 cu.in.) straight-six gasoline engine (albeit with fuel injection) and leaf-sprung rear axle – but it offers a lot of car for the money. In Britain, most 4WDs, although they may be sophisticated in engineering and design terms, do not include too many creature comforts as standard fittings. By contrast, the Cherokee set the market alight with all sorts of goodies all in the basic (and highly competitive) price.

The engine can churn you along at a good pace, and if you use the kickdown, it has vivid acceleration, accompanied by a seductive roar from under the hood. At permissible American highway speeds, the cruise-control works well, but on the faster European road network, you wouldn't think you had 184bhp on board, and the automatic transmission hunts up and down the ratios in an effort to keep your speed up. The 2.5 liter (152.5 cu.in.) straight-four version available is frankly not powerful enough at 122bhp, and certainly takes a lot of the fun out of the Cherokee.

TOP TEN SPECIFICATION:
JEEP CHEROKEE

ENGINE:
In-line straight-six or four, iron barrels with fuel injection

CAPACITY OPTIONS:
2.5-liter (152.5cu.in.), 4.0-liter (244 cu.in.)

TRANSMISSION:
Four-speed automatic with two-speed Command Trac part-time transfer case

SUSPENSION:
FRONT: *Live axle, four links, coil springs and Panhard rods*
REAR: *Live axle, leaf springs, gas dampers*

STEERING:
Power-assisted recirculating ball

BRAKES:
Ventilated front disks and rear drums with ABS

BELOW
The Cherokee, perfectly at home again in Australia, quieter but more thirsty than some other models of transport.

Off-Road Capability

Off-road this is less of a problem. With the Cherokee spearheading Jeep's return to various countries around the world, the need for serious off-roading could not be escaped. For example, it has just gone back into the Australian market after ten year's absence, and there you need a workhorse that can do 300 miles (500km) a day on rough roads in the outback. On sandy or dusty tracks, the Cherokee can charge along, its suspension giving a remarkably smooth ride. And, if you have the powerful air-conditioning up to pressurize the cabin, you don't get any heat or dust into the comfortable interior, allowing you to press on for hour after hour with a minimum of fatigue.

The only drawback in the outback is the need to find fuel, since the Cherokee's engine does have a wicked thirst; surprisingly, the 2.5-liter option is only a little more abstemious. The answer to the problem may lie with the new 2.5-liter (152.5 cu.in.) turbo-diesel engine that is now going into the front of the Cherokee's two boxes. The Italian VM engine was once found in the Range Rover, but this new unit is considerably more modern than that and meets all current emission legislation while at the same time giving enough power and torque to keep everyone satisfied. It may look ordinary and a little unsophisticated, but the Jeep Cherokee is in there with a shout.

LEFT
In dusty conditions, whether in the West or Australia, it is best to keep the air-conditioning on full to pressurize the cabin and keep the dust out.

JEEP GRAND CHEROKEE

For grand occasions

BELOW

Even more full of luxuries than the Cherokee, the Grand features everything as standard, including the indispensable drinks holders.

The Cherokee has been an incredibly popular vehicle, but market research showed that it had one drawback: it lacked a V8 engine. There wasn't room for one under that hood, and anyway, Chrysler wanted to build something different: softer-looking with rounded edges. The Grand Cherokee is still recognizably a Jeep Cherokee shape, but it is now much more than that.

It is already a major success in the U.S. and is being built in left-hand drive form in Austria for Europe, with a right-hand drive version to follow for the 27 percent of the world that drives on the left. Whereas the Cherokee uses leaf springs at the rear, the Grand has coil springs all around. While the Cherokee has selectable two- or four-wheel drive, the Grand has permanent four-wheel drive. And where the Cherokee has a 4.0-liter (244 cu.in.) straight-six engine, the Grand Cherokee has a 5.2-liter (317 cu.in.) V8 that puts out a manly 212bhp at 4750rpm.

Handling Characteristics

The Quadra Link rear suspension has a tendency to sway around a little in urban areas, but it improves at speed. In any case, the European version has firmer suspension to cope with the more twisting and undulating roads. Permanent four-wheel drive helps the vehicle to corner with limited body roll, and it controls the power noticeably better than the Cherokee in two-wheel drive, which can readily be persuaded to wheelspin and fishtail all over the place on wet asphalt.

TOP TEN SPECIFICATION:
JEEP GRAND CHEROKEE

ENGINE:
V8 gasoline, fuel injected

CAPACITY OPTIONS:
5.2-liters (317 cu.in.)

TRANSMISSION:
Three-speed automatic, selectable overdrive, full-time four-wheel drive, two-speed transfer case

SUSPENSION:
FRONT: *Live axle with coil springs*
REAR: *Quadra link with live axle, coil springs*

STEERING:
Power-assisted recirculating ball

BRAKES:
Front and rear disks with ABS

RIGHT
Grand Cherokees are now built in Europe, although they lack the chrome trim that you see here on the American models. Same vehicle, different tastes.

The power unit is delightful – the characteristically mellow V8 delivery that makes the Japanese V6 engines seem revvy and irritating by comparison. With 285lb/foot of torque at 3050rpm, you don't need to rev this block; just let it rumble away to itself as the scenery flies by. Mated to a three-speed automatic with selectable overdrive, you don't have much to do apart from press the loud pedal, although there is a disappointing amount of slack in the torque-converter, which it is wise to remember when pulling out of junctions.

Creature Comforts

Inside you get good-quality leather, excellent air-conditioning, an air-bag for the driver, and a host of ancillaries as standard. The plastic, particularly for the glove compartment, could be better, but overall the interior seems spacious and well-reasoned, and there is plenty of room in the rear for all your luggage. The suspension keeps most of the bumps and thumps away from the cabin, the engine growls quietly to itself, and there is minimal wind noise coming in. This is a fine vehicle for covering the distances.

And it doesn't matter if you are on-road or off it. The live axles front and rear give fine articulation on the rough, letting you get over all sorts of obstacles, while the torque and soft power delivery give you traction even on slippery surfaces without the need to resort to electronic gadgetry. This is an honest, easy-to-live-with vehicle happy in any environment. What more could you ask?

MERCEDES-BENZ

G-WAGEN

A very accomplished off-roader

It must have seemed like a good idea at the time. The Range Rover was creaming sales all over the world in the 1970s and had created a market for sophisticated off-roaders with style. Surely, then, the people in Stuttgart reasoned, the market was ready for a Mercedes-Benz off-roader. The logic was impeccable – but things didn't quite work out that way, and sales over the last 20 years or so have been unremarkable if you take away orders from various armies and government agencies around the world.

Top-Quality Engineering

This is a shame because the Merc is actually extremely good – although first you have to get used to those looks, which many observers have said look better in camouflage paint rather than thick gloss. Underneath is something different, although there are marked similarities to the Range Rover, such as permanent four-wheel drive and coil-sprung live axles front and rear. The things that set the G-Wagen (Geländewagen) apart from every other off-roader, though, are its feel and quality.

ABOVE

Attention to detail and excellent taste mark the Mercedes G-Wagen interior.

BELOW

The Mercedes-Benz off-road ability has seen it taken up by both military and governmental agencies around the world.

TOP TEN SPECIFICATION:
MERCEDES-BENZ G-WAGEN

ENGINE:
Straight-four diesel or straight-six gasoline with fuel injection

CAPACITY OPTIONS:
3.0-liter (183 cu.in.) for either gasoline or diesel

TRANSMISSION:
Four-speed automatic with two-speed full-time transfer case and lockable centre inter-axle differential, with cross-axle differential locks front and rear

SUSPENSION:
FRONT: *Live axle, coil springs, radius arms, and Panhard rods*
REAR: *Live axle, coil springs, radius arms, and Panhard rods*

STEERING:
Power-assisted recirculating ball

BRAKES:
Front and rear disks with switchable ABS

BELOW
The G-Wagen is the only mass-produced light utility four-wheel drive to have front and rear differential locks. Their correct use can aid the experienced driver in the toughest conditions, but whether they are absolutely necessary has been the subject of much debate.

Engine Options

Sitting in the leather seat of a G-Wagen produces a unique sensation that is achieved by the German factory doing things differently and doing them superbly well. Doors close with a heavy clunk, every single button and switch has been perfectly made, and the use of leather and wood is exemplary – good, thick stuff, too, unlike the trim used in some of the Japanese upscale off-roaders. It is like sitting in a German boardroom, rather austere but excellent taste with real attention to detail.

On the road the G-Wagen drives very well, with a certain amount of body roll on the corners held in check by hefty anti-sway bars front and rear. There are various engine options, both gasoline and diesel, their one similarity being sophisticated delivery of reasonable power. The 300GE, for example, uses a 3.0-liter (183 cu.in.) straight-six gasoline engine producing an adequate 170bhp at 5500rpm. Like most

BELOW
A Mercedes-Benz in the tough stuff – just the time when those diff locks may come in handy.

LEFT AND RIGHT
The G-Wagen is available in both three- and four-door body styles, although it is the three-door that has proved the most popular.

of the units used, this comes from the Mercedes car line, and both power and torque (173lb/foot) are delivered perhaps a little higher up the rev range than would be ideal in an off-roader.

Differential Locks

But off-road the G-Wagen has several tricks up its well-tailored sleeve. Axle articulation is good, although it isn't up to Range Rover levels; approach and departure angles are superb, helped by the lack of overhang at front and rear. What really work, though, apart from the steady power delivery, are the three rocker switches on the dashboard. These control differential locks for front, rear, and center. Axles can be made to wave about in the air, in conditions where many others would be stuck, but switching in and out of the relevant diff-lock will transfer drive to the wheel on the ground. The G-Wagen will keep going over severe terrain as long as the driver knows which button to press and when. You would have to be unlucky to get stuck in a G-Wagen anywhere in the world.

It's expensive, different, and a very accomplished off-roader. But, above all, it is a Mercedes-Benz.

BELOW

Permanent four-wheel drive and coil-sprung live axles front and rear mean confident driving over any terrain.

AM General Hummer

A general to follow

BELOW

Forward visibility, thanks to a short, sloping hood, is good, but in extreme conditions it still makes sense to have someone outside checking the route.

As the laws of both nature and economics start to bite into vehicle design, even 4WDs are beginning to look more and more like the same two-box design with rolling edges. You couldn't say that of the Hummer. It comes in hard- and soft-top versions and is a crowd-pleaser and center of attention whatever its configuration. It looks tough, and its association with violence, in the hands of the military, is probably more of a turn-on than a turn-off.

Now the Hummer is available to civilians and is used by organizations like the U.S. Forestry Service and the National Park Service. It has been in production since 1985 as a military 4WD. In army spec, it is defined as a High Mobility Multi-Purpose Wheeled Vehicle (HMMWV) – whence its popular name, Humvee or Hummer. In action all over the world, most notably during the Gulf War, it has proved that it is capable of looking after itself, shrugging off aggression, not just from enemies, but from heavy-handed GIs.

ABOVE

Hummers come in various options, from two-door to four-door, from soft-top to hard-top, but all of them are BIG.

ABOVE

It feels scary and looks dramatic, but it takes more than this to stop a Hummer.

Civilian Spec

It has proved so popular that by the time makers AM General's military contract ran out at the end of 1994, more than 100,000 Hummers had been made. Currently it is sold to the military, to non-military government services, to small businesses, and to the outdoor fraternity. Five civilian models are available: two- or four-passenger hard-top, four-passenger open canvas top, two-passenger industrial fleet hard-top, and four-door wagon. All were introduced at the beginning of 1993.

All versions have the hefty 6.2-liter (378 cu.in.) Detroit diesel that speaks with a menacing growl. But, to be honest, its bark is worse than its bite: it develops a meager 150bhp, which propels this 5,000-pound (2270kg) lump only up to about 65mph (105kmh) top speed. Acceleration is also leisurely through the GM Hydramatic three-speed automatic, but you get the feeling that, once you press the accelerator, nothing in the world is going to stop you from getting up to speed.

BELOW
About the only thing that will stop a Hummer is if the trail is too narrow. This was no problem for the Jeep, but the Hummer didn't have much room to spare.

ENGINE:
V8 diesel

CAPACITY OPTIONS:
6.2-liters (378 cu.in.)

TRANSMISSION:
Three-speed automatic primary transmission with two-speed full-time transfer case

SUSPENSION:
FRONT: *Double short and long arms, coil springs, double-acting hydraulic*
REAR: *dampers*
Double short and long arms, coil springs, double-acting hydraulic dampers

STEERING: *Power-assisted recirculating ball*
BRAKES:
Inboard hydraulic disks front and rear

BELOW
Rod Hall flying high in the Baja. Hummers have won the production class in the Baja desert races. They may not be the fastest, but the build quality and design wins every time.

On- and Off-road Performance

Because the Hummer was designed to get through anything, from desert to arctic conditions, and from deep water to light gunfire, ground clearance had to be a massive 16 inches (406mm), which was achieved by using offset geared hubs so that the center line of the entire drive train was raised. This doesn't do much for the interior space. In addition, its 1.92:1 reduction gears double the torque at the wheels where you need it most, enabling Hummer to get over terrain that would break a lesser vehicle.

Interestingly, the Hummer is so civilized and easy to drive that you don't get the impression that it was built for soldiers. The auto box is smooth in operation and allows the diesel's massive engine braking to work for you on steep descents. There is a lot of torque so that you don't need to rev the motor to get up even steep slopes, while the sheer bulk of the vehicle helps damp out bumps and thumps. The incredible width, more than that of a Ferrari Testarossa, makes even 40-degree side-slopes negotiable, and the overall effect is like sitting in your living room while the scenery goes by.

The Hummer conveys a feeling of massive strength, like a bull, along with the impression that it is a real handful to drive. The reality is that it is very strong, but anyone can drive one comfortably. You don't need to convince Arnold Schwarzenegger — he owns three Hummers!

3

Soft-tops and Fun 4WDs

Into leisure mode

There is, as we've already said, a wide variety of reasons for the success of 4WD. One of the easiest to understand is that they are FUN. In particular, the models that have come to the market with open tops have specifically appealed to the young – and the young at heart. Even in Europe, where the weather cannot compete with California's, soft-top 4WDs have found an eager and enthusiastic market.

It's difficult to place specific credit for this pheno-menon, but one manufacturer does spring to mind when looking at the European scene. Whereas the Jeep, now in its latest Wrangler manifestation, has had a successful following in the United States, it was Suzuki who looked at FUN and decided it was more than just another optional extra for the 4WD: it was to come as standard equipment on its vehicles.

European and American Success

The Suzuki SJ and Samurai "jeep" models that hit Europe during the early 1980s were gaily painted fun machines, the most successful of which were open to the elements with their removable rag tops. These models were originally introduced to the North American market wearing Chevrolet badges. The success of this Japanese model led to General Motors and Suzuki signing a joint production agreement, and an assembly plant was established in Canada. Models for the European market were being built in Spain, which certainly made the Suzuki SJ a world 4WD.

BELOW

Suzuki's SJ and Samurai series brought 4WD to a great many new enthusiasts who were struck by the chance to run small, gaily painted machines built for fun.

RIGHT AND BELOW

The British market was shown the Suzuki X-treme as a design exercise based on the Vitara at the 1994 International Motor Show in Birmingham, England. The public's response was so great that a limited run of 500 vehicles has been produced.

The Roadholding Scare

There then followed a bizarre period where Suzuki SJ models came under fire on both sides of the Atlantic from consumer organizations. The claims were that these little machines were potentially dangerous because they were more prone to roll over than other 4WDs. No 4WD multipurpose vehicle, of course, should be expected to handle like a conventional passenger car when driven on the road. In Britain, this led to Suzuki producing an informative booklet on how to drive the SJ, and in American showrooms, every Samurai had a prominently displayed notice which read: "It won't spoil the fun knowing that the Samurai handles differently from an ordinary passenger car. Avoid sharp turns and abrupt maneuvers."

4WD Street Cred

It certainly didn't seem to spoil the fun of Suzuki enthusiasts. When the Samurai was replaced by the European Vitara model in 1988, it was obvious that the Japanese manufacturer was keen to keep the wind blowing through the hair of its owners. This led to the Vitara Sport becoming an essential fashion accessory for European "bright young things." This fashion phase has led to a huge aftermarket industry, offering Vitara owners ultrawide alloy wheels and tires, and bright shiny bull bars that look capable of deflecting herds of buffalo, yet are more often than not made of brightly colored, deformable plastic (to keep the consumer groups at bay). Fancy colors and flashy graphics have become all the rage. Suzuki

launched its new 4WD on the North American market as the Suzuki Sidekick or, under the General Motors brand name, as the Geo Tracker. The model has proved a sales success whether called Vitara, Sidekick, or Geo Tracker. There is even a North American version of the Tracker available with 2WD!

Upping the Power

If that appears a little strange, swallow this. Geo is the Chevrolet division of General Motors, and obviously the guys in the development shop didn't feel that the Tracker's 1.6-liter (97.6 cu.in.) fuel-

FUN 4WD SPECIFICATION:
SUZUKI VITARA/ GEO TRACKER

ENGINE:
Four-cylinder, SOHC, fuel injection

CAPACITY OPTIONS:
1.6-liter (97.6 cu.in.)

TRANSMISSION:
Five-speed manual with two-speed part-time transfer case; or four-speed automatic with two-speed part-time transfer case

SUSPENSION:
FRONT: *Independent MacPherson struts, coil springs*
REAR: *Coil-sprung live axle*

STEERING:
Recirculating ball. Power-assisted option

BRAKES:
Front disk, rear drum

In the U.S., the Suzuki is built under license as the Geo Tracker – ironically, there is even a two-wheel drive version.

injected, four-pot gasoline engine was really Chevrolet material. They decided to elbow this engine out and replace it with a 3.4-liter (207 cu.in.) V6 from the Camaro sports car! This was then coupled to the four-speed automatic transmission and 4WD system from a Chevy S-10 pickup. Certainly this is a "don't try this one at home, children" type of conversion – it emphasizes the enthusiasm that these small soft-tops can generate. (Or maybe they serve some pretty strange coffee in Chevy's staff cafeteria!)

LEFT AND BELOW

General Motors entered the European four-wheel drive market with the Frontera, with models like the Sport and the four-door appealing to a wide range of people.

Combined Operations

Cross-continental pollination is evident throughout the automobile industry, with major manufacturers combining to produce joint projects. Interestingly, General Motors has not limited its corporate favors to one Japanese manufacturer. Besides its link with Suzuki, GM is partnered with Isuzu, which has led to one particular model which in the past few years has had a major impact in the European market.

Called the Isuzu Rodeo in the U.S. and the Vauxhall Frontera in Britain, it bit deep into a previously untapped consumer area. While the Suzuki Vitara Sport has been successful in Britain, it has tended to be a single's vehicle. The Rodeo, however, fed into the family market — and the Sport version, since it is larger than the Vitara Sport, has taken a firm grip of fun-loving family 4WD enthusiasts!

In many ways, both these models have a similar design philosophy. Besides both having removable tops, both have the bulging wheel arches that give it that popular "tough guy" appearance.

FUN 4WD SPECIFICATION:
JEEP WRANGLER

ENGINE:
Six-cylinder, SOHC, fuel injection

CAPACITY OPTIONS:
2.5-liter (152.5 cu.in.), 4.0-liter (244 cu.in.)

TRANSMISSION:
Five-speed manual with two-speed part-time transfer case. Or three-speed automatic with two-speed part-time transfer case

SUSPENSION:
FRONT: *Hotchkiss-type multileaf springs with dual-action telescopic dampers*
REAR: *Hotchkiss-type multileaf springs with dual-action telescopic dampers*

STEERING:
Power-assisted recirculating ball

BRAKES:
Front disk, rear drum

Jeep's Wrangler design owes much more than a little to the original Willys products. In this shot, its off-road ability owes much to the driver.

Enter the Wrangler

When it comes to tough, you can't get more so than the quasi-military Jeep Wrangler. With its bright color schemes and massive, fully padded roll cage (allowing passengers to get a better grip when standing up and cruising), the vehicle's World War II looks have been no disadvantage to sales. Neither has the vehicle's modern-day Meccano construction technique, which allows for doors to be removed and the front screen folded down to get the full force of the wind in your hair. But it's fun!

Vehicles like the Wrangler have had their imitators, none more so than recent offerings from the Third World, such as the Mahindra from India and the Asia Motors Rocsta. The Mahindra has had a deservedly tough introduction to Europe's 4WD market with its late-1940s look and build quality to match. The Rocsta, on the other hand, comes from South Korea and has impressed many observers. Along with the Ssanyong, the Asia Motors Rocsta confirms that the Koreans are coming along to the 4WD party with some interesting new options.

ABOVE

No, this is not a Wrangler, but a Rocsta from Asia Motors of South Korea.

LEFT

The Koreans are definitely going to have a say as to who has a share of the 4WD market. Besides the Rocsta and the Ssanyong, the Kia Sportage is new to Europe from 1995.

LEFT AND RIGHT

It's fair to say that it was the Japanese manufacturers who first developed the small, cheap 4WD market, so it is no surprise that the new Toyota RAV4 should be an innovative new development of that theme.

Japanese Novelty

Imitation may be the sincerest form of flattery – but it's far more interesting when something completely new comes around. So we conclude this chapter with the latest offering, again from Japan, but this time from Toyota.

The Toyota RAV4 caused quite a stir on its introduction to Europe in late 1994. Its radical shape had been seen before, Toyota introducing it at motor shows as far back as 1988. Many commentators can

be forgiven for thinking that it was just another concept vehicle that would never see the light of day as a production model. But how wrong they were. This is yet another development of the four-wheel drive market aimed firmly at those to whom image is all-important.

First views of a RAV4 produce the reaction that the glass panels should be removable for full open-topped effect. In fact, they are stationary, but the vehicle does have two large sunroofs which, when removed, can be clipped to the rear door. Clever, that.

Road-car Spec

It is when you look underneath this obviously image-conscious body that a few more interesting details appear. The suspension features MacPherson struts at the front and double short and long arms at the rear. The engine, a multivalve 2.0-liter (122 cu.in.) fuel-injected, four-cylinder, comes straight from Toyota's sedan car range. It drives all four wheels through a five-speed transmission with not a transfer box in sight, so it makes no pretence at any mud-plugging ability. Such specification will lead you to guess correctly that the RAV4 excels on the road.

Take the RAV4 off-road, and the lack of a low-range transmission and limited wheel articulation from those road-proven MacPherson struts limits your options. It's capable, but when the going gets muddy, it's no match for the likes of the Vitara/Tracker, with which it competes for showroom sales.

So, does this mean that the new choice of fun 4WDs is more concerned with image than off-road ability? Let's hope not. For all its good looks, the RAV4 would probably be just as successful if it only drove its rear wheels. To fully appreciate the 4WD phenomenon, enthusiasts will want to make sure that vehicles remain as capable off the road as on it.

FUN 4WD SPECIFICATION:
VAUXHALL FRONTERA

ENGINE:
Four-cylinder, fuel injection

CAPACITY OPTIONS:
2.0-liter (122 cu.in.), 2.4-liter (146.5 cu.in.)

TRANSMISSION:
Five-speed manual with two-speed part-time transfer case

SUSPENSION:
FRONT: *Independent torsion-bar-sprung short & long arms*
REAR: *Leaf-sprung live axle*

STEERING:
Recirculating ball

BRAKES:
Front disk, rear drum

LEFT
Cue music, cue the Beach Boys – and girls! Four-wheel drive has been a success because it is FUN, and long may it remain so.

Pickups, Utes, Trucks, and Rigs

Big Rigs

Pickups are the biggest pick-me-up of the biggest market in the world. Utilities – utes, trucks, call them what you like – are the most commonly bought vehicle in North America. And what is good news for home-based producers is that customers are buying American trucks. In the past few years, the Big Three – Chrysler, Ford, and GM – have been completely re-defining the way in which vehicles are built, sold, and maintained, and they now look leaner than they have for decades. In the last couple of years, the value of GM's stock has risen more than 120 percent; but even that is feeble compared to that of Chrysler, up over 400 percent in the same period. And it's mainly down to trucks, where the profit margins are as big as the sales.

"Buy American" Trend

In 1993 both Ford and Chrysler lost money on their car sales, but returned hefty overall profits because of their truck sales. The Japanese have been slow to capitalize on this development in the market, and have been hindered by import tariffs and a growing "buy American" sentiment. Vehicles like the Toyota T100 have not really taken off, partly because they haven't had great big torquey V8s under the hood – but that may change when this model is made in America in 1996. Most other Japanese manufacturers are simply re-badging American models, with limited success. It looks like being something of a turkey shoot for the American big boys.

This is a market as big as the vehicles themselves. At one end, you have some battered old GMC pick-up with a dog and a gun rack, and at the other you have monster trucks leaping over and then crushing rows of cars in a stadium – a highly symbolic form of entertainment.

Extreme Rigs

The mid-size truck sector is a massive one, but it is in the full-size market where most of the extreme rigs hang out. GMC started it, when it created the Syclone, a rig that had gone the big-block, lowered-to-the-wheels route, making it the fastest vehicle – truck or car – in GMC's inventory.

BELOW

The GMC Syclone can carry a flat-bed full of sand, but it can also kick sand in the face of just about any other vehicle on – or off – the road.

TECHNICAL SPECIFICATION:
FORD SVT LIGHTNING F-150

ENGINE:
Small-block V8 tuned by Ford Special Vehicle Team

CAPACITY:
5800cc

POWER:
240bhp at 4200rpm

TORQUE:
340lb/ft at 3200rpm

LENGTH:
197.1 in. (500cm)

WHEELBASE:
116 in. (295cm)

HEIGHT:
74 in. (188cm)

GROSS WEIGHT:
3980 lb. (1805kg)

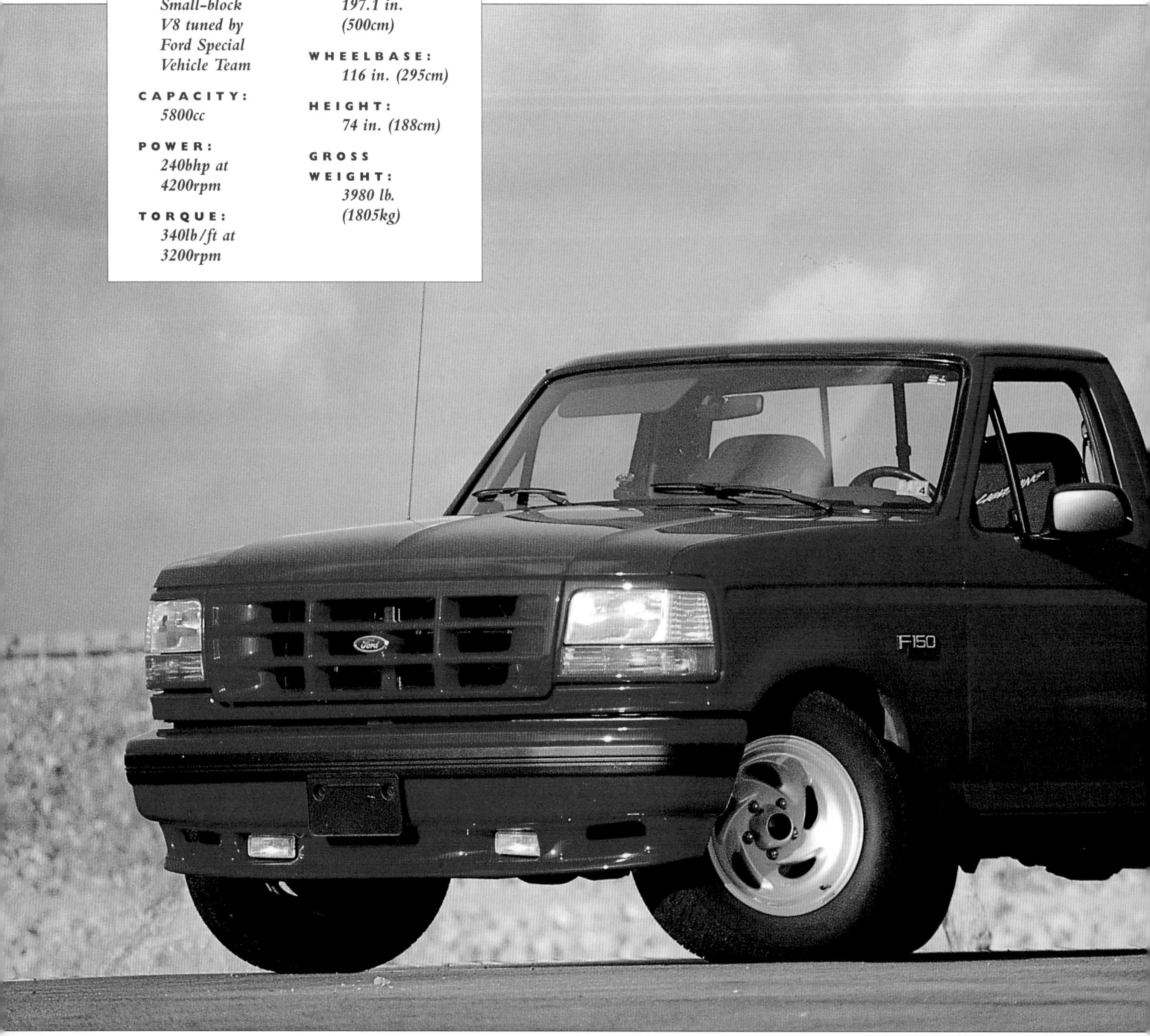

ABOVE

Ford's Special Vehicle Team took a stock F-150 full-size pickup and injected it with steroids and testosterone.

A company as big as Ford was not going to take that without retaliation. The Lightning started life as a placid-looking F-150, one of the biggest-selling pick-ups around, with sales in some years of around half a million units. Then Ford's Special Vehicle Team got cranked up and transformed it into a monster, with a 5.8-liter (354 cu.in.) V8 up front cranking out 240bhp and enough torque to wrinkle the black top – 340lb/foot. at 3200rpm. Tweaks like lowering the body, adding stronger shocks and more of them, and fitting bigger anti-roll bars and tires all helped to make the Lightning controllable, but you still have to be quick with the counter-steering if you want to keep the flat-bed behind you.

BELOW

The F-150 Lightning puts out 240bhp and can smoke its fat Firestone tires on the way to doing 0–60mph in 7½ seconds.

The Dodge

Both these vehicles were pretty special, but you can always count on Americans to go one step further. And it would of course be Chrysler that did it, one of the most imaginative automobile corporations around. It came up with the Dodge Ram. The sheer scale of the bulbous thing is pretty impressive, although that can be beaten by the big F-Series Fords. What really sets it apart is the all-aluminum 8.0-liter (488 cu.in.) V10 that fills the front end. Taken from

the Dodge Viper supercar, where it turns out 400bhp, it has been detuned to give a measly 300bhp and a pitiful 450lb/foot of torque at 2700rpm.

The looks of the big BR3500 are something else, too, and are the result of a vice-president at Chrysler saying "Let's say to hell with it and do what we want." That is a startlingly brave move for a big corporation, but it not only shows the way Chrysler is moving now, it shows the company was right. Sales are through the roof for a production truck, not some tricked-up one-off.

The Dodge Ram 2500 in full Laramie SLT specification, full-size luxury.

The amazing thing about trucks like the Dodge is how user-friendly they are, with Club Cab versions that can comfortably seat four, yet with a cargo area that has had the tailgate widened to allow a camper shell to slide in easily. As time goes on, you pay a smaller and smaller price in terms of inconvenience and impracticality for owning something that can act as both a car and a truck, and yet it can also go out and whip the field in anything from drag racing to desert racing.

TECHNICAL SPECIFICATION:
DODGE RAM

ENGINE:
*90-degree cast-iron
V10, liquid cooled
with multiport
injection*

CAPACITY:
8000cc

POWER:
300bhp at 4000rpm

TORQUE:
450lb/ft at 2400rpm

LENGTH:
224 in. (569cm)

WHEELBASE:
135 in. (343cm)

HEIGHT:
75.9 in. (193cm)

GROSS WEIGHT:
3990 lb. (1810kg)

**TOWING
WEIGHT:**
6168 lb. (2798kg)

LEFT
*The most extreme of the
many Ram variations is
the 3500-series with
double wheels at the rear
under hugely flared wheel
arches.*

ABOVE AND BELOW

Stadium racers put out almost as much power as an Indy car, but are geared to do only about 60mph.

Stadium Racing

As you can see elsewhere in this book, pickups regularly win punishing desert races like the Baja 1000, but similar-looking vehicles regularly entertain stadium crowds for indoor racing. Like true racers, the vehicles are made of space-frame chassis with glassfibre panels fastened over, and a massive V6 or V8 somewhere in the middle. Watching them leap over the obstacles, flying high above you for seconds at a time, then thudding down to earth without destroying themselves, is quite a sight.

And driving them is no easy feat, despite the fact that you have an automatic and maybe only three gears. On some circuits, the vehicles stay in one gear the whole lap, but with an engine that puts out 500-600bhp yet is geared to have a top speed of about 60mph, you can imagine the acceleration you have to contend with on a loose surface. And let's not forget that you haven't got the circuit to yourself either.

This isn't a form of racing that has gotten outside the U.S. yet. But since Europe is already besotted with indoor stadium motocross, it may well take to this most sensational of car sports as well.

Mid-engined Toyota stadium racer shows why you need that much suspension movement. Rod Millen and Ivan Stewart have both won many races for Toyota in the stadiums.

Monster Show Trucks

One sport that England in particular probably doesn't have enough room for is the monster truck displays, which started with the Ford Bigfoot and just got bigger and bigger. In the U.S., there is an instinct to go bigger, in a big country. Millions of rigs have been lifted, usually by lifter kits that raise the bodywork by about 4 inches (100mm), but for extreme mud, where you need excellent ground clearance, or in some rocky scenarios, where you need the best approach and departure angles, you can be looking at an everyday vehicle that has been lifted by more than a foot (300mm).

To make that happen, and to accommodate the massive tires that need to be extra-wide to help compensate for the loss of stability, you have to look at everything. Leaf-sprung vehicles are more difficult to repair than coil-sprung live axles. But each type of vehicle is going to need attention to everything, from the line of the driveshaft as it angles up into the higher transfer case, to installing longer brake lines, and a steering kit to restore the steering to its original geometry. Do it wrong or on the cheap, and you'll wish you'd installed a roll cage.

Show Truck Championships

The show trucks – those monster trucks that draw the biggest crowds – compete most of the year in various championships throughout North America, like the Jamboree Nationals. These trucks run on truly immense tires, taller than a man, and are fitted under rigs that have been raised several feet. You wouldn't want to try a high-speed slalom course with them, but they are perfect for drag racing over series of obstacles that include anything from bumps to elderly Cadillacs. And the mud bogs are just perfect for them to wallow in, with their height keeping them above the goo, while the tires act as flotation chambers, churning across the mud like a Mississippi stern-wheeler rather than sinking deep into it. Crazy? Come on, guys – this is America!

LEFT AND BELOW

Well, what would you do with a monster truck? Car crushing is a spectacular "monster" show.

LEFT

Monster drag race meetings certainly pull in the crowds.

4WD Taken to Extremes

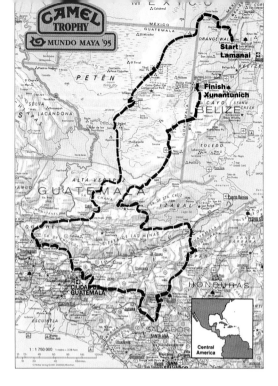

LEFT

Off-road in a big way! This is the route plan for the 1995 Camel Trophy that takes the contestants and their specially-prepared Land Rover Discoverys through Belize, Mexico, Guatemala, El Salvador, and Honduras on 1,000 miles of real adventure.

Hot:

The Spirit of Adventure –
the success of the Camel Trophy

After fifteen years, the Camel Trophy has successfully established itself as the ultimate international challenge for 4WD enthusiasts. Some of this success has been due to the enormous American marketing machine that has promoted the Camel brand around the globe, but much more is due to the concept of the event and how that encapsulates what 4WD sport is really all about.

In simple terms, the Camel Trophy is an opportunity for non-professional 4WD enthusiasts to represent their country and battle through a variety of tasks in some of the wildest, most inhospitable areas of the world. Every year, each competing country holds a selection process to find the two best off-road drivers to represent them.

RIGHT

When it comes to the Camel Trophy, the Discovery is undoubtedly the world's best off-roader.

LEFT

In 1989, the Camel Trophy used the Land Rover 110 – the vehicle's longer wheelbase allowed for more passengers …

The event itself sees this wide variety of drivers from all over the world, driving Land Rovers for 1,000 miles (1,600km) of serious off-road adventure. Along the route, the organizers run a number of special tasks, with each national team fighting hard to win enough points to bring home the coveted trophy. But it is more than just a competition, since without the united effort of all the teams pulling together – quite literally at times! – the off-road Land Rover convoy would never make it to the finish.

Off-road Cooperation

It is really this need for all the teams to work together off-road that is the heart and soul of the event. And once you have experienced a Camel Trophy – as both authors of this book have done – you are a fully converted off-roader.

Each year, the convoy's routes are planned in advance – but this is often done before the rainy season. By the time the Camel Trophy contestants arrive, the monsoons (or whatever) will have done their worst, and any rough tracks that might have been there before may have been washed away. At times, progress can be alarmingly slow: trees have to be winched out of the way, and local vehicles dragged

out of the mud. Part of the Camel Trophy training given to contestants before the event includes a crash-course in bridge-building. Over the years, drivers have often been forced to build temporary structures that allow the vehicles to cross terrain that has been scarred with torrential rain and rock falls. More often than not, rival teams have to help each

ABOVE

Accidents can happen, even on Camel Trophy. It's actually all part of the grand plan, since the convoy has to work together constantly to succeed across the difficult terrain.

In 1982, the Camel Trophy organizers used Range Rovers – a fact that pleased many of the indigenous members of a local four-wheel drive club.

other through the toughest sections, and we can report from experience that those tough roll cages are tested to the limit as some vehicles spend time on their backs with all four wheels waving in the air.

The Camel Trophy has driven through Sulawesi (Indonesia), Malaysia, Brazil, Argentina, Chile, Paraguay, Madagascar, Australia, and even the wastes of the Russian steppes. Through them all, the Land Rovers have performed admirably. After all, this is 4WD country.

What better way is there of testing your four-wheel drive vehicles than on events as tough as this?

WHAT MAKES A TROPHY 4WD VEHICLE?

The first Camel Trophy was contested in Jeeps, but the Amazonian rain forest proved more than a match for these vehicles. Since that first event, the Trophy has been the sole prerogative of the Land Rover. Initially this was with the 90 and 110 models; later, the competitors were offered rather more comfort with the Range Rover; the most recent events, however, have used Discoverys, which have proven to be the world's best off-road "Camel."

This is Sulawesi, Indonesia, in 1988, and the Swiss team is not colliding with a mountain as first appears, but gingerly traversing a bamboo and log bridge that the Trophy convoy had just repaired.

Standard Production Models

What is perhaps not realized, however, is that these machines compete in relatively standard form. They are the models you can go and buy in the showroom. The modifications permitted are strictly controlled. They include a comprehensive roll cage, incorporating a roof rack needed to carry all the provisions and fuel to keep the convoy going. Another modification is the installation of an engine snorkel to allow the vehicle to breathe when wading through the many deep rivers encountered en route. Finally, the underbody is protected by a skid plate, and each vehicle is equipped with an all-important winch. Apart from that, the Camel Trophy vehicles are as they roll off the Solihull production line at Land Rover's headquarters near Birmingham, England.

Cold:

To New York via Siberia–
Ford's Overland Challenge

It is often the case that off-road enthusiasts overrate the ability of 4WD vehicles. You know the kind of thing: the driver is convinced both he and the vehicle are invincible – with the inevitable result that over-confidence and poor judgment see him get well and truly stuck. Well, Ford's 1994 London-New York Overland Challenge looked rather like that even before the vehicles had set off from London. Backed by live television broadcasts, standard Ford Maverick and Mondeo 4WDs were to attempt something never done before and that was to drive across Europe, Siberia, the Bering Strait, Alaska, and the rest of North America, to finish on the steps of the United Nations building in New York – and coincide with the launch of Ford's Mondeo sedan car in the U.S.

LEFT
Ford took its Mavericks and four-wheel drive Mondeo road cars to New York via Siberia and some of the world's most inhospitable terrain.

Trial by Cold

When planning the event back in the warmth and comfort of the marketing department's luxury offices, this probably all seemed relatively simple – an interesting exercise in logistics. The true enormity of the task is difficult for anyone to comprehend. By the time the convoy arrived at Bering Strait at the easternmost point of Siberia, the team had traveled some 15,000 miles (24,000km) across some of the most inhospitable terrain on earth, with temperatures at times dropping to about -60°F (-52°C).

As you might expect, those temperatures caused great problems for the Maverick 4WDs. Despite this, the preparation of the vehicles was noticeably simple. Apart from underbody protection, additional jacking points, and all the fuel and brake lines being routed inside the vehicles, the only unusual piece of equipment was 3Kw Eberspacher truck heaters.

Across the Ice to Alaska

Such a high-profile "media event" was a risk for Ford, and in the end it backfired. However, this was not because of the failure of the 4WDs. The Mavericks made it all the way to the edge of the Bering Strait, where they were to be carried over the frozen water and ice fields in a tracked Arktos amphibious machine. Unfortunately, the Arktos threw a track and broke a half-shaft, and so the Mavericks had to be flown across to Alaska in Hercules transporters.

It is also fair to mention that on several occasions the Mavericks had to be given a tow by multi-wheel-drive Russian Ural trucks when the snow became too deep to allow the Fords to make forward progress.

Uncharted Routes

It must be borne in mind that the Mavericks were going where no other mass-produced, commercially available vehicle had ever been. All drivers on the event spoke of the surprise shown on the faces of local inhabitants when they looked at these funny little machines. These people were more used to massive, tracked military vehicles, not standard road-going cars.

The company's faith in these vehicles was great – some would say too great. Most cold-weather testing of ordinary road cars is done at temperatures down to -35°F (-37°C), and as we have said, this expedition took them further than that. Unwisely, Ford had neglected to secure data on what would happen to the 4WDs at temperatures below this point. At times, plastic items like door handles became so brittle they snapped. The vehicles had to be kept running overnight. Even so, on one occasion the moisture in the exhaust froze, blocking the exhaust pipes and stalling the engines. It needed severe jump starts the next morning – but start they did.

And the Maverick 4WDs made it to the United Nations building on time. The only real worry for the drivers on the final stages was the risk of being arrested for speeding on the 4,500-mile (7,250km) blast across North America!

Cold:

Roughing it in Ukraine

The Warn Transylvania Trophy

The world has seen many events – rallies, raids, races – rushing all over it, from the well-established Paris-Dakar to the Paris-Moscow-Beijing, which has been run just once – but these are for professional teams with big budgets. The Transylvania is contested for by amateurs using an extraordinary array of vehicles, from Mercedes G-Wagens with the doors taken off to aging Toyota Land Cruisers and brand new Land Rover Discoverys. And, since it it an event sponsored by an American winch company, you just know it isn't going to be high speed down well-trodden tracks all the way.

ABOVE

One of the better "tracks" in the Ukraine.

Sure enough, the event struggles through some of the most backward and remote areas of Ukraine. There are no roads, only a few logging tracks. There are no towns, only tiny villages with no electricity, no running water, and inhabitants who have often never left the locality in their lives.

Modified G-Wagen, making waves on the Warn Transylvania Trophy.

Plowing Through Endless Forest

The first event was rather like the Camel Trophy in organization, but the second, in 1994, was more competitive, with several days requiring racing from dawn to dusk. Mind you, some of the "racing" was done at about 2mph (3kmh) as vehicles had to winch themselves up muddy slopes through the endless forests. Winch discipline broke down as Germans, British, Dutch, and other nationalities tried to get to the top of gullies first, winch wires crisscrossing each other and tempers fraying.

This went on for more than a week. In between the winching, vehicles would get up to speed on long, open fire breaks or on one of the compacted paths that might connect one village with the next. Choking dust or cloying mud were the only alternatives as it was either parched or pouring, and the trees stretched to the horizon in every direction. Camping at night, washing in freezing streams just a few hundred miles south of Chernobyl, cooking over open fires, the contestants started to look like the locals.

The event shows signs of evolving and maturing, and has already started to attract entrants of the caliber of Heinz Plotz, winner of the Munich-Marrakesh in 1990 with his heavily modified Suzuki. But it would be a shame if it didn't keep that door open for the wacky privateers in their even wackier vehicles. The Ukranians didn't know what hit them.

LEFT
American Jeep tears through a Ukranian firing range – the Russian armored vehicle in the foreground has definitely broken down.

ABOVE
Heinz Plotz and his highly modified Suzuki – to change gear in the river, you had to find the gear lever by feel under the water.

Hot:

Hot Rocking

Jeep Jamborees

Jeep safaris and jamborees are part of the American outdoor life. You take off into the mountains or the swamps or the desert, making sure you've got plenty to eat and drink, and get in some serious off-roading with all the family. To Europeans these events seem odd, since in Europe the off-road commodity that you always have too much of is mud. And the oddest of all are those where what you have is rock. Slick rock.

The most famous route is the Rubicon Trail, but there are several routes that are less well known, but just as good. Looking at the array of Jeeps lined up for the Jeep Safari in Moab, Utah, you could have been forgiven for thinking that they were out for a pleasant cross-country doddle. The rigs looked neat and professional – but they were full of couples, the wife with a blanket over her knees, fussing about the flask of hot coffee. This was entirely misleading.

RIGHT
You'd have trouble walking over this terrain, but Jeeps can get through as long as you don't rush it.

LEFT
Jeep Wranglers lead a convoy on the Rubicon Trail.

Lion's Back in Utah, a fearsome climb. You have to follow those tire marks exactly, but turning around at the top makes most people stay very quiet.

Rock Climbing on Four Wheels

Off-road hereabouts the rocks stick up like bald domes, there's scant vegetation, no earth, nothing. And you just drive up them, up gradients where you would swear that gravity was going to beat you. All the rigs run tires almost as soft as slicks, with huge ground clearances to keep the chassis away from the hard surface. They inch down what look like sheer cliffs, often so steep that it is only your hands on the wheel and your feet on the pedals that are touching the vehicle. Even your behind is out of the seat and all you can see is iron-hard rock. This is tough on diffs, hubs, and everything else, so you need a strong rig to survive. But, if you do, you'll never feel the same again about off-roading. Other off-road routes may be faster or muddier, but nothing can get your heart beating as fast as this.

BELOW LEFT
Catering on the Rubicon Trail is about hearty fare – a pancake mixture is prepared with huge industrial drills.

BELOW
Jeep CJ5 rock-hops on the trail – note the huge, soft tires to give traction on the slick rock.

Hot:

Desert Storms
The Baja 1000

This is one of the oldest and toughest off-road races, and has been run every year since 1967. The badlands of southern California and northwestern Mexico are an inhospitable wilderness of desert, salt lake, and razor-backed mountains. Through this, the competing trucks and motorbikes will be traveling at up to 120mph (190kmh), and the pace is so hot and the terrain so terrible that normally only about a quarter of the starters actually cross the finish line. As one competitor put it, after hours of daylight and darkness, sun, and rain: "This course sucks." Because the course – 750 or 1,000 miles (1,200 or 1,600km) depending on the route – is so extreme, the vehicles have to be, too. Disregarding the bikers – who must surely be certifiable to even think of taking part – the racers display an amazing diversity, with trucks to match. Where else would you find works Hummers with drivers of the caliber of Rod Hall? You get everything from British racers in Land Rovers – Brit John Saxton won his class in the 1994 event in a converted 110 Land Rover – to the professionals like the legendary Ivan "Ironman" Stewart. Ivan is around 50, but he won the event outright in 1994 in his PPI Toyota SR5 lookalike. Most teams run a driver and navigator, if only because you then have someone to help when you crash or get a puncture. But Ivan Stewart does it all on his own.

ABOVE
Ivan "Ironman" Stewart tears through the desert in his V6-engined Toyota pickup. He will be in bed asleep by the time the last racers trail in behind him.

RIGHT
Little more than the silhouette is standard on this Jeep Cherokee desert racer, driven here by Englishman Darren Skilton in the Baja 1000.

LEFT

Challenges come in all
shapes and are tackled at
all speeds. This Jeep
escaped without even
damaging the paintwork.

BELOW

With over 700bhp and
more than two feet of
suspension movement,
Ford F-150s are ideally
suited to racing over rock
or sand at over 100mph.

Power Aplenty

Top rigs are simply space-frames with pickup or simi-lar body parts fastened to them. Underneath there are up to 30 inches (750mm) of suspension move-ment, multiple shocks at each corner, and engines that put out almost as much as a Formula One or Indycar racer. The big boys are putting down around 780bhp to the wheels, leaping and bucking through the sand, sliding around on the dry salt-lake beds and crashing through rock rubble. It is not a sight for the faint-hearted.

And it's made worse by the locals, about 400,000 of whom turn out around the circuit. They get drunk and wander out into the path of a charging racer – who is never going to back off. Others build traps made up of old bed frames or rocks and a big hole, and wait for a million-dollar racer to hit it, with a gratifying thump and leap through the air. The locals love it, and the crews seem to take it in their stride – instead of having A-10 ground-attack aircraft running ahead of them, which is what many of us would want to do. There is certainly nothing quite like the Baja.

Index